Drive Thru Teachers

McDonaldization of the Classroom Teacher

Bridgette Jackson

Drive Thru Teachers: The McDonaldization of the Classroom Teacher

Copyright © 2012 Bridgette Jackson

All Rights Reserved. Published 2012.

No part of this publication may be reproduced, distributed, or transmitted in any form or by any means, including photocopying, recording, or other electronic or mechanical methods, without the prior written permission of the publisher, except in the case of brief quotations embodied in critical reviews and certain other noncommercial uses permitted by copyright law. For permission requests, write to the publisher, addressed "Attention: Permissions Coordinator," at the address below.

First published by Faith Books & MORE

ISBN 978-0-9860247-8-8

Printed in the United States of America

This book is printed on acid-free paper.

3255 Lawrenceville-Suwanee Rd.
Suite P250
Suwanee, GA 30024
publishing@faithbooksandmore.com
faithbooksandmore.com

Ordering Information:
Quantity sales. Special discounts are available on quantity purchases by corporations, associations, and others. For details, contact the publisher at the address above.

Orders by U.S. trade bookstores and wholesalers. Please contact Ingram Book Company: Tel: (800) 937-8000; Email: orders@ingrambook.com or visit ipage. ingrambook.com.

Acknowledgements

This book is dedicated to my mom and dad. Thanks for being the best cheerleaders in my life.

Contents

Introduction		7
Chapter 1	The Facts	15
Chapter 2	Efficiency	29
Chapter 3	Calculability	41
Chapter 4	Expecting the Predictable	51
Chapter 5	Who Is in Control?	63
Chapter 6	Recommendations	73

Introduction
McDonaldization 101

Introduction

Today the golden arches of McDonald's restaurants attract millions of customers on a daily basis across the world. The convenience of a hamburger, fries, and a milkshake served to you at the drop of a hat just the way you like it is the McDonald's way. **"I'm lovin' it!"**

McDonald's does not just serve you a meal; it serves you a dream. Its commercials appeal to our utopian hope of the perfect family with great food in our bellies and *happy-go-lucky* lifestyles. In the book, *McDonaldization* Revisited, the authors write, "McDonald's success is based upon its ability to tell a story, a story that does not make sense from a logical perspective but rather an esthetic one" (Alfino, Caputo, Wynyard, 1998). Regardless of the state of America's economy and skyrocketed unemployment rate, McDonald's continues to offer its customers friendly smiles and a fun atmosphere.

McDonald's is, by far, one of the most successful businesses in the world. So how did this empire begin? How has it maintained such a dominant presence?

The McDonald's empire was established in 1940 by Dick and Mac McDonald who introduced the *Speedee Service System*. Modernizing the concept of the fast food restaurant, the *Speedee Service System* capitalized on principles, systems, and practices of food delivery first introduced by the founders of the White Castle restaurant chain who used the same system between 1923 and 1932.

Dick and Mac McDonald licensed the first site in 1953 and subsequently sold a franchise license to Ray Kroc in 1955. Kroc opened his first McDonald's in Des Plaines, Illinois, near the city of Chicago, on April 15, 1955. On that same day, he incorporated his business as McDonald's Systems, Inc. later renamed McDonald's Corporation.

Ray Kroc was an astute businessperson. He recognized the enormous potential of the fast food franchise. The McDonald's *Speedee Service System* was based on the principles of "high speed, large volume, and a low price... a process known as the *fast food factory*" (Ritzer, 2010). The McDonald's business model allowed Kroc to dominate the fast food industry, creating one of the most successful franchises in the world. By 1959, Ray Kroc had opened 68 restaurants and was experiencing phenomenal growth.

Many corporations, both for-profit and non-profit, have adopted the McDonald's business model because it helps them reduce overhead and increase earnings (Ritzer, 40). Today the aroma of low wages and low overhead even permeates many school buildings across America. The resulting stigma that now rests on the teaching profession *is hard work for little compensation*. That is the McDonald's way.

The philosophy behind the McDonald's business model has infiltrated many aspects of our American way of life. Its influence can be felt to the far recesses of our subconscious minds. This philosophy is called McDonaldization, the process by which the principles of the fast food restaurant dominate our society (Ritzer, 2010).

Over the last three decades McDonaldization has made its presence known in the school system, and not always in a positive way. Its four main ingredients are: efficiency, calculability, predictability, and control.

Efficiency refers to satisfying a need and providing gratification through a series of predesigned steps. The drive-thru window

Introduction

is an example of efficiency. It allows customers to receive their food as quickly as possible.

Calculability deals with the quantitative aspects of the business, the idea of "a lot for a little." The Dollar Menu is an example of calculability.

Predictability allows a customer to receive the same service and quality no matter which location they visit. In other words, for the consumer, there are no surprises. A Big Mac in Idaho tastes the same as a Big Mac in the Big Apple.

Control limits a variety of details: the number of items on the menu; the way associates perform their duties; how management interacts with associates; and even the type of lighting found in each franchise. All elements are carefully controlled (Ritzer, 15).

The McDonald's influence has spread to the farthest parts of the world. The golden arches can be seen in some of the most distant countries. McDonald's serves its customers one drive-thru visit at a time; yet the effects of McDonaldization have overtaken the masses.

This same philosophical approach regulates today's school systems; and it shows no signs of leaving classrooms any time soon.

The franchise is not just a brand—it is a way of life. Customers enjoy a sense of control when their wishes are fulfilled in under five minutes. They can have pickles, no pickles, mayonnaise, no mayonnaise or "fries with that" just for the asking. In addition, these pre-planned choices are provided with excellent service and a bright smile. Regardless of how meticulous or belligerent, the customer is always right.

In like manner, teachers have been turned into customized workers who must meet the meticulous demands of unrealistic policies, angry parents, and tightly controlled conditions.

Kroc's empire has grown through smart advertising strategies using media—including television, movies and the internet—to reach consumers. These outlets appeal to children who make up a sizeable portion of McDonald's customer base. Eric Schlosser, author of *Fast Food Nation*, said, "They (McDonald's) perfected the art of selling to children. They study the fantasy lives of young children, and then apply the findings in advertisements and product designs" (2001). Focusing on children assures almost instant access to parents or guardians. This creates multiple customers while only advertising to one age group—adolescent youth.

Adolescents can be easily persuaded and influenced. Their process for selecting clothing, hairstyles, and even what they want to eat tends to be greatly influenced by emotion and the dictates of pop culture. None of their major influencers take into consideration calories, nutrition, much less safety. Schlosser continues, "Hundreds of millions of people buy fast food every day without giving it much thought...They rarely consider where this food came from, how it was made, and what it is doing to the community around them" (2001).

Children can be influenced—by entertainers, musicians, and prestigious television figures—to believe that fast food is good for you regardless of the facts about its contents. Many children enter school buildings on a daily basis with these images in mind. Regrettably, the persons left to combat these influences by helping children think for themselves—the opposite messaging of McDonaldization—are teachers.

Introduction

After several decades, McDonaldization has spread like a virus and its influence has penetrated public school cafeterias. "Food produced by McDonald's and other fast-food restaurants has begun to appear in high schools and trade schools; over 50% of school cafeterias offer popular name-brand fast foods" (Ritzer, 11). Many children prefer the taste of fast food over that of homemade meals and advertisers are fully aware of this. "America's schools now loom as a potential gold mine for companies in search of young customers" (Schlosser, 2001). The idea of "give it to me now the way I want" will sit on-site in schools across the nation as students enjoy the convenience fast food offers.

Schools house one of the largest targeted markets for fast food retailers. The ability to sell to grade school children during school hours greatly expands their sales potential. A merger between fast food retailers and schools yields unbelievable profits for all parties involved.

The convenience of fast food promotes instant gratification—an ideology firmly ingrained in the American psyche—and the vehicle is McDonaldization. Some refer to this phenomenon as "microwave mentality." From this view the idea that "patience is a virtue" is frowned upon. In a McDonaldized society it is difficult for children to understand the merits of patience, diligence, and working your way to the top. They want what they want and they want it now. Dazzled by the entertainment industry and envying famous entertainers' lifestyles, which have also become McDonaldized, many children feel they do not need school because they will one day *make it big.*

When observing the entrance of McDonaldization into the school setting we must consider its psychological effects on the way children and parents view teachers. We must examine the lack of trust evidenced by the interactions of high school administrators with classroom teachers, the roles of parents and communities in academic life, political involvement in the performance of teachers' duties, and the impact of each of these on the classroom. These relationships have all been permeated by McDonaldization and, ultimately, classroom teachers bear the brunt of the pressure.

Although McDonaldization can be seen as a means to an end, it can be extremely challenging to schoolteachers. The focus of this book is to illustrate how the principles of McDonaldization have crept into school systems across America. Instead of creating teachers who feel supported, respected, and financially rewarded, America has produced what I like to call *Drive Thru Teachers*.

Driven by the principles of efficiency, calculability, predictability, and control, teachers all over the nation are overworked, undercompensated, and made to pay the penalty for the mistakes of the education system as a whole.

Although the principles of McDonaldization work to help companies save money and increase their "bottom line," their effects on teachers can be tremendously negative. The repercussions of which I write are not based on theory, but drawn from the stark realities of many thoroughly disillusioned teachers who have left the field prematurely.

CHAPTER 1

The Facts

The Facts

As we explore the McDonaldization of classroom teachers, it is important to understand which factors fuel the philosophy. These facts and statistics should stimulate conversations among parents, community leaders, educators, and policymakers alike. The facts should alarm and motivate participation in the implementation of change. They paint a picture of everyday teachers, their livelihoods, and the conditions and philosophies that make their profession so uniquely challenging.

Composition of Teachers in the Field

In 2007-2008:

- There were 3.5 million teachers in America.
- The majority of elementary, middle, and secondary school teachers were female.
- The racial/ethnic backgrounds of teachers were 83% White, 10% Black, and 7% Hispanic.
- Approximately 28% of teachers had 20 or more years of teaching experience, down from 37% in 1999-2000.
- The average experience was 14 years, down from 15% in 1999-2000.

Source: The National Center for Education Statistics, Indicator 27 (2010).

These indicators show that approximately one-third of the teacher-workforce was in the high school setting and predominantly female. On average, teachers—both male and female—have 14 years of teaching experience. Most teacher pay scales go up to approximately 30 years of experience.

Although 14 years of experience is considered mid-journey, the majority of teachers are tenured. Most veteran teachers have retired, being replaced by younger teachers with little or no experience.

Racial/ethnic statistics show a lack of diversity among teachers with the majority being white females. Respect for diversity is a performance indicator upon which teachers are evaluated; however, diversity is not often reflected in who is hired to teach.

The Financial Benefits

In 2008-2009:

- The average annual income for public school teachers was $53,910.
- In the lower 10th percentile, elementary teachers earned $33,830; middle school teachers $34,360; and high school teachers $34,600.

In 2010:

- Teacher salaries were 14% below salaries of other professionals with comparably complex skill sets.
- The salaries of public school teachers in many states have been outpaced by inflation over the past decade. Cost of living and variance in teacher pay from state to state are factors.

Sources: US Department of Labor, 2009; The Economic Policy Institute, 2010; US Department of Education, Rankings and Estimates: Rankings of the States 2009 and Estimates of Schools Statistics 2010, National Center for Education Statistics, 2010.

Compensation remains one of the greatest areas of discontent among teachers and one of the primary reasons they exit the field. Beginnings teachers with zero or very few years of experience make up the lower 10th percentile of the pay scale. With salaries in the low $30,000s, many potentially qualified candidates refuse to enter the field for this very reason. Taking into consideration inflation and cost of living, these salaries do not attract as many potential candidates as our schools require. Unless a teacher has been in the school system for at least ten years adequate financial rewards can be far out of reach.

In today's U.S., economy low-income teachers feel doubly strained by the recession. Many are taking on multiple part-time jobs. Statistics suggest that teacher salaries are keeping up with inflation, yet there are school districts all across America in which teacher pay rates have remained frozen since the 2008 financial crisis while out-of-pocket costs have increased. If there have been no increases in pay for teachers to compensate for corresponding rises in cost of living then teacher pay must be re-evaluated.

New Hires

In the National Center for Education Statistics' 2005 *Special Analysis Report*, "new hires" were defined as transfers from one school to another, teachers who left and returned to the profession, delayed entrants who were not enrolled in school but were not yet working in the field (including career changers), and recent college graduates.

Note these 1999-2000 statistics:

- Of working teachers, 17% were new hires.
- Among new hires 57% were career changers who had never taught in a school setting of any kind.
- New hires were likely to be young and teaching out-of-field rather than continuing teachers.

Many new hires come into teaching from other industries/fields of work with no previous teaching experience. Many have little knowledge of what to expect in the field. Some are not competently trained to enter the classroom prior to their first day of school.

New hires tend to be young, recent college graduates thrown into the worst classrooms. According to the Alliance for Excellent Education (August 2005): "Beginning teachers are particularly vulnerable because they are more likely than their more experienced colleagues to be assigned low-performing students. Despite the added challenges that come with teaching children and adolescents with higher needs, most new teachers are given little professional support, feedback, or demonstration of what it takes to help their students succeed."

As older educators retire, younger, inexperienced ones enter the profession. These teachers are not prepared to deal with the realities of the classroom, including heavy workloads and increased responsibilities. The teaching contract severely understates the actual duties required. Teacher trainings across America must do a better job at properly informing new applicants of the workload involved. Providing truthful, up front information could greatly increase the longevity of those individuals choosing to enter the field.

Career changers who enter education, for the most part, lack the skills to meet the demands of high-needs children. Experienced teachers, on the other hand, have acquired these skills over time; yet, experienced teachers tend to stay with upper level, advanced placement (AP), and honors classes. These levels present less discipline problems with far fewer classroom management issues than high-needs classes.

It is not uncommon for high-needs classrooms to be overcrowded with students who are problematic, have repeatedly failed to pass, or are close to aging out. High-needs children need experienced teachers who have the capacity, skills, and patience a novice teacher may not initially possess.

Teacher Evaluation

Teacher evaluations are both formative and summative. Formative evaluations provide teachers with feedback on how to improve performance and enhance their teaching practice. Summative evaluations assist administrators in making final decisions about salary, tenure, personnel assignments, transfers, or dismissals. Other evaluation methods are observation, lesson plans, self-assessments, portfolios, student work samples, and achievement data (e.g., Barrett, 1986).

A study by REL Midwest was conducted in December of 2007 on teacher evaluation policies from the states of Illinois, Indiana, Iowa, Michigan, Minnesota, Ohio, and Wisconsin. The results of the study highlight the following:

1. Administrators are the most common evaluators (e.g. principals and assistant principals).
2. Only one third of the policies detailed how to communicate the evaluation process and procedures to teachers. Many districts felt teachers needed to refer to their teacher handbooks, their contracts, or their new teacher orientation documentation.
3. Most of the policies required teachers to sign the evaluation after review.
4. Many districts did not have policies in place to address the procedures for assessing teachers who had previous unsatisfactory evaluations.

5. Less than one of ten policies required evaluator training.

Sources: Examining District Guidelines to Schools on Teacher Evaluation policies in the Midwest region, REL Midwest, Brandt et al., 2007).

Ideally, the purpose of evaluations is to optimize teacher performance in the classroom, increase student achievement, and bridge the gap in achievement between racial/ethnic and socioeconomic groups. They also serve as a mechanism to exit unqualified professionals from the field.

There are collections of research-based studies supporting different teacher evaluation methods; however, most researchers agree that a combination of methods and tools provide a comprehensive approach.

A teacher's livelihood swings on the hinges of evaluations. However, evaluations tend to be more subjective than objective. The evaluator comes into a classroom at a specific moment in time that will never be lived again. Thus, the resulting observation is only a temporary snapshot of what is actually occurring in the classroom throughout the day.

According to the statistics of the REL Midwest report, less than 10% of evaluators (usually administrators) are trained to perform the evaluation. So how do administrators know what to look for? Performing observations, for the most part, is learned by trial and error.

Walk-through observations, or observations under fifteen minutes, have limited effectiveness because unless conducted on a consistent basis they restrict the observer from making a fair assessment of a teacher's classroom.

Findings of this study also show a breakdown in communications between administrators and teachers following the observation.

The Facts

The goal of evaluations is to build upon positive qualities and support student achievement as well as to improve teachers' "areas of weakness" (i.e. professional development classes). An *ongoing* interchange between evaluator and teacher is necessary to discuss where improvement must occur and what classes or trainings are available to assist in that area. A conversation about areas of strength and areas of opportunity informs the teacher as well as the administrator on what steps to take in terms of professional development (Brand et al., 2007).

When post-observation dialogue is missing teachers must interpret the meaning of evaluators' notes. Often teachers misinterpret the recommendations. As a result, they may show minimal or no progress in strengthening their areas of weakness.

What happens if a teacher does not agree with an evaluation? What happens if there is a negative evaluation without conversation? It is not rare for administrators or principals to ask teachers to sign evaluations after a short conversation or none at all. For the administrator, the goal is to meet the deadline for the evaluation and turn in the appropriate paperwork. Little or no consideration may be given for the type of class being evaluated; for example, an honors class versus a high-needs class ripe with discipline problems.

A holistic evaluation approach is indispensable to maintaining fairness in the evaluation process. Countless times a teacher fully disagrees with an evaluation, but feels pressured to sign the document because the paperwork is due. Paper pushing is a significant problem in the teaching profession.

Teacher Turnover

Teacher turnover is the process of teachers exiting the field ("leavers") with new hires filling those vacancies on an annual basis. The 2005 *Special Analysis Report* states:

1. Between the school years 1999-2000 and 2000-2001, public schools lost 15% of their teachers due to various reasons; retirement, family, transfers, and miscellaneous other factors.
2. Teachers in high-poverty public schools were about twice as likely to move to another school as their counterparts in low-poverty public schools (10% to 5%).

The 2000-2001 Teacher Follow-up Survey (TSF) (from the 2005 *Special Analysis Report*) showed that of the 15% of teachers overall who exited the field:

1. Retirement accounted for 20%.
2. Family reasons, pregnancy, and child rearing accounted for 30%.
3. The desire for better salaries and/or benefits accounted for 14%.
4. Desire to pursue a different kind of career accounted for 13%.
5. Among the "leavers," the five most commonly reported sources of dissatisfaction were:

    (a) Lack of planning time—60%

    (b) Too heavy a workload—51%

    (c) Too many students in the classroom—50%

    (d) Too low a salary—48%

    (e) Problematic behavior of students—44%

The Facts

Retirement is a natural progression phase in any career; however, when it comes to teacher attrition, the main reasons for leaving were factors other than retirement.

There tends to be a higher turnover rate among teachers in high-poverty schools than in low-poverty ones. New teachers placed in high-needs classes are more likely to quit due to the rigors and challenges of the environment. Younger teachers tend to be placed in unreceptive, antagonistic environments with children who exhibit discipline problems.

In the first week of school, how should a new teacher react to a child who refuses to cooperate, uses extreme profanity, gets into physical altercations, or acts out because of family issues? New teachers need proper training to assess the needs of each child and to apply the most proven practices to meet those needs. This kind of training should come from practical demonstration and application taught by mentors and master teachers.

In the 1999-2000 school years, the National Center for Education Statistics conducted a "Public School Teacher" survey. In the findings, 67% of teachers who had been formally mentored by another teacher reported that it "improved their classroom teaching a lot." Mentorship provides guidance and cultivates creativity.

With no clear understanding of how to handle student conflicts, many teachers simply walk out of the classroom or transfer to another school. The National Education Association conducted a study on teacher turnover and reported that close to 50% of new teachers left the profession during the first five years of teaching because of poor working conditions and low wages (March 2010).

Teacher turnover is not a new concept; American schools are

experiencing a teacher shortage due to this phenomenon. The president of the National Education Association, Reg Weaver, said: "We must face the fact that although our current teachers are the most educated and most experienced ever, there are still too many teachers leaving the profession too early, not enough people becoming teachers and not enough diversity in the profession" (Washington Post, 2006).

Many young teachers are disenchanted with their pay in comparison to the unrealistic demands placed on them. It is a fair statement that people want to feel properly compensated for their work. When there is not comparable pay for work rendered turnover is almost inevitable. The Bureau of Labor Statistics reported: "Because of the high dropout rate of younger teachers there will be plenty of job openings for teachers over the next 10 years."

When these teachers leave, the children suffer. Teachers exiting the field leave behind classes subjected to a series of substitute teachers. The most disturbing fact here is that many substitutes are expected to teach subjects in which they are not proficient. They act as warm bodies or babysitters. The result is a discernible impact on student learning and achievement.

Heavy Workload

Teachers carry other responsibilities besides preparing lessons and grading papers. These may include a variety of the following:

1. Supervising children on campus before and after school
2. Lunch duty/playground duty/hall duty/bathroom duty
3. Classroom management
4. Writing personal growth plans for areas of improvement

The Facts

    on which to focus

5. Possible mentorship of new teachers
6. Coaching sports
7. Participation in district communities which set learning standards
8. Preparing personalized education plans for students not performing at grade level
9. Participation in special education meetings and giving feedback on individualized education plans and 504 plans for exceptional children
10. For leading teachers, conducting meetings for teachers in their content area and establishing common planning
11. Assisting guidance departments in preparing report cards for mailing
12. Conducting parent-teacher conferences
13. Attending professional development classes
14. Working with parent and community organizations
15. Assisting administration in conducting surveys for teachers, parents, and students
16. Assisting administration in school improvement plans
17. Attending staff meetings after school
18. Administering and/or proctoring state tests for tested courses

Teachers are responsible for more than just their classrooms. They are expected to lead in the overall well-being of their school and its students. Schools are communities within the community at large. A single teacher may not be responsible for every one of these additional duties; however, a majority of teachers are responsible for several of these. It is no surprise that many teachers feel overloaded, especially new ones.

As cited by the Alliance for Excellent Education, the 2004-2005 MetLife Survey of the American Teacher stated, "New teachers reported being greatly stressed by administrative duties, classroom management, and testing responsibilities, as well as by their relationships (or lack thereof) with parents" (Issue Brief, August, 2005). Teachers need relief to focus on what is most important—their students.

The statistics in this chapter reveal all the factors that play an integral role in the McDonaldization of the K-12 teacher. It is clear that American teachers are overloaded with paperwork, have little support, and handle heavy workloads. These stresses are similar to fast-food workers expected to work hard, receive little compensation, and serve with a smile. In addition, McDonaldization calls for management to hand down policies to subordinates with little or no collaboration or input from the team.

With the four main principles of McDonaldization—efficiency, calculability, predictability, and control—the American school system is penetrated by the "give it to me the way I want" mentality. In the following chapters, we will explore each of these principles, discuss how they have infiltrated the school setting, and describe the possible consequences if immediate changes are not implemented.

Chapter 2

Efficiency

Efficiency

In this chapter, we will address the teacher and each stress factor that causes interference despite the demands for efficiency in the classroom. These stress factors are: (1) lack of mobility, (2) excessive workload, (3) curriculum issues and complex scheduling, and (4) administrative and political pressures.

As defined in the introductory pages of this book, efficiency is about satisfying needs and providing gratification by following a set of predesigned steps (Ritzer 15). Teachers are required to be efficient by following a state-prescribed curriculum and by adhering to materials in predesigned pacing guides.

Multiple factors interfere with the teaching process. "Professional factors that have been identified as being highly stressful for teachers are: disruptive students, excessive paper work, curriculum issues, complex scheduling, burdensome workload, environmental pressures, administrative entanglements, lack of mobility, and other less significant factors" (Gold & Roth, 18).

Lack of Mobility

According to the Alliance for Excellent Education, most beginning teachers are assigned to classrooms with high percentages of at-risk children who perform below grade level (August 2005). In low-performing classrooms, disruptive behavior is a natural by-product of teaching high-needs populations.

Many new teachers struggle with classroom management simply because of inexperience. With budgetary issues, lack of resources, and little colleague support, being efficient in an impoverished school is tough. Teachers who have both the experience and the credentials to teach low-performers prefer not to work with this troubled student population. Well-credentialed teachers are often assigned to honors and advanced courses. Younger generations of teachers feel stuck teaching low-performing classes.

The stress from a full day of low-performing classes alone causes many teachers to leave the field. It is a known fact that, "Schools with a higher percentage of poor students have greater difficulty retaining teachers" (Broughman & Rollefson, 2000; Ingersoll, 2001; pp.16-17).

In difficult classroom environments plagued with student misbehavior, teacher turnover is inevitable. Substitutes are often unqualified to continue teaching the abandoned classes with the same level of expertise. Thus, the children suffer and fail to receive a complete education.

Teachers assigned to difficult classes tend to be limited to these settings throughout their careers while teachers assigned to advanced classes tend to remain at that level. There are trends to the student-teacher matching process. In *Evaluating and Rewarding the Qualities of Teachers: International Practices*, Sclafani quotes Lankford and Loeb: "There is good reason to believe that the student-teacher matching process is more than just a theoretical concern... A significant amount of research in the U.S. shows that more advantaged students, in terms of family income and parental education, tend to be assigned to higher-quality teachers, as measured by such characteristics as experience, degree level, and test performance" (132).

The regularity with which veteran teachers are assigned academically gifted and higher-income students and newer teachers are assigned struggling lower-income students is an epidemic. This type of teacher-student matching creates a *glass ceiling effect in teaching*. The glass ceiling keeps novice and growing teachers from experiencing the full continuum of student populations. They are consistently assigned to lower performing and underprivileged student populations. The flipside of this process affords the more seasoned teacher the opportunity to teach high performers or academically gifted students. These teachers experience little to no serious behavioral issues, which automatically exposes "better teachers" to higher marks on evaluations in multiple areas including classroom management. This same principle dooms teachers struggling in challenging classrooms to the lowest marks.

In Daniel Duke's book, *Teaching – the Imperiled Profession*, he states: "The rigors and emotional demands of teaching might seem much less enervating if teachers knew that every few years they would undertake a different set of responsibilities" (143). Perhaps more teachers would be willing to work with below-grade-level performers if their assignments were varied. This would provide all teachers the opportunity to grow in the profession and to work with diverse groups of children of varied abilities and talents. There can be no efficiency in classrooms across the board if the same teachers are experiencing burnout and stress due to problematic classes. "Teachers are demoralized and dissatisfied, feeling they are not leading productive or meaningful professional lives. Stress is a major factor in producing this condition" (Gold & Roth, 3).

The glass ceiling must be removed and teachers—both veteran and novice—must share in the challenges of teaching problematic and low-performing classes. If the glass ceiling effect persists, younger generations of teachers will continue to turn over at even higher rates then they have historically.

Excessive Workload

The duties of teachers extend beyond what most expect when they enter the field. Unless student teachers experience a variety of schools with children of all populations, most will be unprepared for the classrooms they enter. In *Teacher Burnout in the Public Schools,* author Anthony Dworkin writes, "A large percentage of teachers enter the profession blindly, unaware of the nature of the job and its expectations. Many quit early in their careers…" (65). A realistic view of what the profession entails is not accurately depicted in undergraduate education classes in colleges across America. Education programs should properly prepare students majoring in education as a career choice for the environments in which they will be immersed.

Teachers are required to do more than teach the curriculum. They also supervise students, conduct peer observations for colleagues, mentor new teachers, run after-school clubs, coach sports, complete paperwork on students, create and implement personalized education plans for children performing below grade level, conduct parent/teacher meetings, and tutor, among many other responsibilities. On top of maintaining student work, classroom management, lesson plans, staff meetings, and obliging administrators and principals during evaluation observations, this workload can be extremely challenging. Author Andy Hargreaves writes,

"In recent years, these parts of the teacher's work that extend beyond the classroom have become more complex, numerous and significant. For many teachers, work with colleagues now means more than structured staff meetings or casual conversations. It may also involve collaborative planning, being a peer coach for a partner, being a mentor for a new teacher, participating in shared staff development, or sitting on review

committees to discuss the individual cases of children with special needs" (14).

Collaboration has become a part of the planning process and is now one of the standards in teacher evaluation practices. Teachers must maintain their domain while being active in the broader learning community. Although this is quite necessary, all these responsibilities add to the amount of time teachers must spend off the clock, away from their families, and uncompensated for the additional work performed.

Curriculum Issues and Complex Scheduling

Standardized test scores have become a topic of great interest over the last seven years. Many teachers question whether they are truly effective in determining the educational and developmental progress of a child. The fact is that all children learn differently and standardized test scores do not work well with every learning style.

There are three main types of learners: visual, auditory, and kinesthetic/tactile. A visual learner is one who must see things written down; an auditory learner must hear things repetitiously, and a kinesthetic/tactile learner must be involved in a hands-on manner and work out problems themselves (Kelly 116).

In addition to these three learning styles, we must also take into consideration children with learning disabilities. These students often require more assistance in the classroom than mainstream students do. A few of the most commonly known learning disabilities are dyslexia (difficulty in processing language through reading, writing, and speaking), dyscalculia (difficulty in math), and dysgraphia (difficulty in writing and organizing ideas). Some of the most challenging learning disabilities classroom teachers face are Attention Deficit Hyperactivity Disorder (ADHD) (inability to stay focused, seated, and on task) and autism (difficulties in academics as well as social challenges).

How can one standardized test give a summative view of a population of such diverse children? Yet teachers are expected to prepare students of all learning styles and levels for one state-mandated test.

Children with ADHD may have trouble sitting through a three-to-five-hour exam. It is a difficult requirement for them to remain seated and focused for that length of time. Added to this is the pressure they may already feel knowing this one test can determine whether they are promoted to the next grade or held back. Children with dyslexia dread taking reading exams and may read or write numbers backward. Students suffering from dyscalculia may feel uncomfortable taking a standardized test, but remain silent to prevent being perceived as "different" from their peers. Regardless of all these unique situations, teachers are expected to perform during the eight-and-a-half-month school year and produce consistently high-test scores.

In *Fast Food Nation*, Eric Schlosser commented: "*Grades (and students are observed by this quantifiable measure of education) might be derived from a series of machine-graded, multiple-choice exams and posted impersonally, often by number rather than by name. In sum, students may feel like little more than objects into which knowledge is poured as they move along an information-providing and degree-granting educational assembly line*" (161).

This pressure to create "assembly line children" is very significant for educators in the sense that they must pour information into students, thereby theoretically producing knowledgeable, critical thinkers able to be propelled into society on a timely basis.

The model of the school system "propelling" children through their learning experience toward a diploma has shown itself to be utterly ineffective. Educators have an unrealistic amount of curriculum to cover in a very short amount of time. It is not surprising that children struggle to add, subtract, multiply, and divide even throughout their high school experience due to the speed at which the curriculum is taught.

Teachers are pressured to cover large amounts of material to prepare students for state (standardized) tests. Yet in recent years, many teachers have found themselves reprimanded for "teaching to the test." This should come, as no surprise when so much of a teacher's worth is dependent upon the results of these end-of-year standardized tests. Test scores can determine the financial future of the teacher and his or her family. After having invested four to six years in pursuing a degree in education, a new teacher finds that one test can determine whether he or she will have to exit the profession and pursue another degree or career all over again.

Heightened concerns around the need to prepare the next generation of students for global competitiveness increases teacher stress. In the book, *Changing Teachers, Changing Times*, Andy Hargreaves states,

"People are always wanting teachers to change. Rarely has this been truer than in recent years. These times of global competitiveness, like all moments of economic crisis, are producing immense moral panics about how we are preparing the generations of the future in our respective nations" (5).

In these hard economic times, with many global issues looming,

Americans are worried about the future. They are asking, "Will our children be able to compete in the worldwide marketplace?" Teachers are under tremendous pressure to perform and to thrust our children into higher levels of academic success.

Every good teacher has an innate desire to see his or her students succeed. However, pacing guides, standardized tests, and time constraints present severe challenges, even to the highly motivated teacher. Predesigned steps restrict teachers from immersing students into the curriculum since some students need more time to learn than do others.

Although several reforms are "on the table" to help give Americans the competitive edge needed to compete in the global marketplace, teachers lack a voice in how they should best be implemented in the classroom.

Administrative and Political Pressures

The pressure to reform and revolutionize the educational system has been overwhelming for many teachers. Their lack of voice in the policy-making process perpetuates the ineffectiveness of reforms now occurring in American classrooms. Hargreaves writes:

"Change may look good on paper or an overhead, but in essence, are superficial and only achieve little more than trivial changes in practice... The involvement of teachers in educational change is vital to its success, especially if the change is complex and is to affect many settings over long periods of time. And if this involvement is to be meaningful and productive, it means more than teachers acquiring new knowledge of curriculum, content, or techniques of teaching. Teachers are not just technical learners. They are social learners too" (11).

Enormous pressures from administrators to implement new research and learning theory techniques leave no room for teacher input. The teacher is in the classroom on a daily basis, making decisions, reflecting on what did and did not work, evaluating how to best restructure lesson plans, seeking to motivate, to innovate, and to reach the troubled child with a dire home life.

Each classroom is comprised of unique individuals with singular needs. Policymakers lack the full scope of knowledge and awareness needed to make proper decisions for teachers and student populations. The teacher serves as a bridge between the student and the policymaker.

The roles of teachers are constantly changing based on the demands of *specified points of authority*: new laws, school board members, district superintendents, administrators, and affluent parents. Teachers are required to fulfill their duties while staying on top of the best practices gleaned from new research to help children learn. Hargreaves writes:

"First, as the pressures of post modernity are felt, the teacher's roles expand to take on new problems and mandates though little of the old role is cast aside to make room for these changes. Second, innovations multiply as change accelerates, creating senses of overload among teachers and principals or head teachers responsible for implementing them..." (4).

New research is constantly emerging. New roles overlap old ones, adding to the immense pressure to perform that teachers already feel. The McDonaldization of education's administration has created managers who use the strong-arm policies of the company to control the performance of its employees. The expectation is 100% compliance or else. Many of these policies and reforms do not have the classroom teacher's requests for assistance, feedback, input, or experience in mind. Hargreaves continues:

"Political and administrative devices for bringing about change usually ignore, misunderstand or override teachers' own desires for change. Such devices commonly rely on principles of compulsion, constraint, and contrivance to get teachers to change" (11).

The pressure to be efficient and to comply with the demands of the school's administration has weakened the input of teachers. They are forced to conform to ideologies, formulas, and procedures which "research says" will help a broken education system. In the creation of these formulas and ideologies, one main ingredient has been left out—the teacher's voice.

Principals are used as puppets to push the agendas of upper management despite the growing and pressing needs of the teacher in the classroom. Ignoring the voice of educators has become all too common. In the book, *Understanding and Preventing Teacher Burnout*, Vandenberghe and Huberman wrote: *"Nobody asks for their (teachers) opinion—even though we have known for a long time how important this is"* (200).

The usefulness of the teacher's voice in the decision-making process is critical. The teacher's job is to pursue the complexities of learning and to perfect the craft of educating students. Teachers plan, implement, execute, and reflect on daily practices in order to improve the learning experience of all students. Lawmakers and administrators—long removed from the classroom—lack this daily experience. Moreover, the daily in-classroom experience of educators lights the path to *true* reform necessary for them to teach and inspire the next generation. Teachers need a voice!

When educators feel they do not have a voice it leads to mistrust of administration. This sort of suspicion is a by-product of the infiltration of McDonaldization where administrators

Efficiency

(the managers) are taught to enforce policy and make teachers conform.

Ray Kroc, founder of the McDonald's Corporation said, "We have found out...that we cannot trust some people who are nonconformists...We will make conformists out of them in a hurry...The organization cannot trust the individual; the individual must trust the organization" (Schlosser 5).

As teachers feel forced to cooperate with unjustified and unsubstantiated reforms, lack of motivation and creativity results. Imagine a program originally perceived to be cutting-edge and progressive. After one or two years, that program is stopped and another is instantaneously introduced in its place. What might this type of action do to the motivation and morale of the person who originally spearheaded the program? Such constant change diminishes the motivation of teachers who are told to "move on to the next thing." With a lack of closure to previous versions of a program and without continued observation over an extended period, it becomes next to impossible to assess effectiveness.

The constant influx of new learning theories and methodologies introduced into the educational system has turned the school into a dollar menu. Choose what works for now—what is most convenient and cost effective. In the final analysis, the children pay the real price and America simply cannot afford that bill.

Efficiency in schools, based on the McDonaldization philosophy, forces teachers to follow unrealistic policies, adopt predesigned packages such as pacing guides, and suppresses the creativity and upward mobility of new teachers. These problems must be properly addressed if we are to move forward in education.

Chapter 3

Calculability

CALCULABILITY

The calculability factor validates quantity over quality. Working with irrelevant curricula, lack of resources, a biased and unfair distribution of growth opportunities, and standardized testing, teachers are struggling to produce students with the potential to pioneer in the marketplace versus simply "passing" students who will be able to do no more than just work in the marketplace.

State and national standards determine public school curriculum. School district leaders then turn this information into pacing guides pertinent to each grade level and developmental stages of growth. Pacing guides set the tempo for how each topic is taught over the span of the academic year. These tend to mix a variety of topics resulting in a lack of focus and little or no usefulness in today's marketplace. How many times have teachers heard the phrase, "When will I ever use this?" from their students?

The expectation is that the teacher should cover a vast amount of material within the ten-month school year (excluding holidays). Some contend that a great teacher can cover all of it and more in the time allotted and that an average teacher can cover the majority of it. There is room for disagreement in that. However, the concern should be not only the selection of the material in the curriculum, but also the developmental appropriateness of it. The alarm is sounding for a revolution in the content of curriculum capable of making children ready for careers in the medical field, engineering, civil service, and even entrepreneurship.

The current trend in our society is that people are applying for jobs in which they are not qualified. In a 2010 report, the United States ranked 17th in science and 25th in math out of 34 countries, suggesting there is a definite state of emergency in education (USA Today, December 7, 2010). Given these statistics, the quantity of graduates does not attest to the quality of them.

Although the overall problem with education results in much finger pointing, we have to focus on the real issue: How can we change what is taught to make it relevant to the current marketplace?

In the book, *Changing Schools for Changing Times*, Kerry Kennedy studied the curriculum in Hong Kong schools. Kennedy discusses a document prepared for the United States Congress explaining the human capital theory *rate of return* in its application to education. Government invests into the public school system with the hope that it will manufacture a productive workforce. This productivity generates income to pump money back into the economy to keep it moving forward (Kennedy 6-7).

"Manufacturing..." "Pumping..." "Productivity..." Does this sound like a fast food restaurant to you? Students are going to school; some even attend college or graduate college. Public school students are taught facts and expected to regurgitate them for tests and quizzes. This process produces students who are productive in a job, but not witty, inventive, in the forefront of technology, medicine, and business. How much money can we pump back into the economy if we are not producing innovators?

Considering the inherent problems found in public school education, the only alternative is private or charter schools. Most middleclass families lack sufficient finances to afford a private school education, and charter schools often have waiting lists too long to wait for. Consequently, a disproportionate number of public school students do not graduate and many do not attend college, especially African American males.

Calculability

The sad truth is that the Government's return in investment over the last several decades, although increasing, remains rather low. The return on investment in 1993 for a college graduate was 10% (Kennedy 11). Kennedy continues, *"Learning is at the heart of the knowledge economy – it is how new knowledge is created and new processes invented"* (7). With such a low return on investment, how much creativity and innovation can we reasonably expect from America's graduates?

As a joint effort, leading industries, teachers, and innovators should come together to collaborate on a way to create relevant curriculum. Curriculum should be based on real world experience and scientific in nature so that children become strong, independent thinkers capable of creating solutions to tomorrow's problems. This may sound like a cliché, however, it is true: Curriculum should change as the marketplace changes.

The modern growth theory has become the basis of curriculum reform in Hong Kong. This model does not assume that staying in school for extended years will automatically produce innovation and creativity. It suggests that students need to participate in the "knowledge economy," which uses math, technology, and science to stimulate creativity, innovation, problem solving, and entrepreneurship (Kennedy 11-12). Math, science, and technology are taught to help students develop, which leads to further research and investigation until new ideas are created.

In America, core subjects are taught from a factual perspective, simply pouring knowledge into students' minds. They are then assessed by how much they can recall on a test or quiz. Where is the creativity in that? How does our current education system connect students to current problems in the local and global economy?

The root cause of the teaching and learning problem lies in the way curriculum is laid out for teachers. The goal of curriculum should be the coupling of ingenuity and content knowledge, not content knowledge alone.

Across Asia, this kind of reform is already evolving. The philosophy behind education directly affects a country's economy. Kennedy says, *"In the curriculum proposal reforms in Hong Kong and throughout the Asia Pacific region it is learning and learning processes that are at the heart of school curriculum. In addition, the creativity, problem-solving, and entrepreneurship that modern growth theory requires as the foundation for economic growth are now also embedded in the proposals for school curriculum reform"* (11).

Asian Pacific schools are ahead of American schools by far. They rank in the top five worldwide in both math and science. The positive results of this reform are indicators that American curriculum needs to undergo similar change. Our children should be equipped to pioneer in tomorrow's occupations that do not currently exist.

American children need to be prepared to compete globally, yet they are overwhelmed by outdated information modeling where we have been as a country, not where we are going.

No one is suggesting we throw away all the education material dealing with the past. No! Yet there is a need for educators to explore current topics such as cures for diseases such as cancer and AIDS, reducing consumption of natural resources, and exploring new breakthroughs in technical, electrical, mechanical, and biomedical inventions. These relevant topics will cause students to be curious, interested, and engaged.

The United States' current education system works to create

Calculability

a biased distribution of wealth by producing more "passing" students in urban and low-income neighborhoods. We have to make great learning opportunities available to schools in every neighborhood.

Take the opportunity to visit schools in a variety of neighborhoods with different income statuses. They can be public, private, or charter schools. Take note of the resources available, the use of classroom technologies, and the diversity of the administration. Make comparisons based on the following questions:

(1) How old are the books?

(2) What advanced classes are available?

(3) What is the budget for extracurricular activities?

(4) How does the building look? Is it clean or unkempt?

(5) When was the last visit by the area superintendent?

As you take mental note of these factors, you will discover an unbalanced distribution of school resources. Although there are warm bodies graduating from both affluent and underprivileged schools the quality of the education is far from equal. Nevertheless, as long as there are students graduating from both types of schools the disparity among impoverished schools will remain overlooked.

In the book, *City Schools and the American Dream: Reclaiming the Promise of Public Education*, Pedro Noguera writes: "*Although we may be in a 'new economy' in which many jobs require advanced skills and education (Murnane & Levy, 1996), there is still a need for people who are willing to accept low-status, low-wage work. As long as some schools (suburban and private) are able to generate a sufficient number of academically qualified students for high-skill, high-wage labor, or as* long as such labor can be imported, the failure of low-performing schools does not pose a problem for the economy" (13).

To get a better understanding of what author Noguera is saying let us do a little math. Let us compare graduation rates of two school districts. We will call them District A and District B. Each district has five schools.

Comparing District Successes

Schools	District A Graduation Rates	District B Graduation Rates
School 1	71%	74%
School 2	64%	87%
School 3	72%	52%
School 4	81%	98%
School 5	83%	99%
District Graduation Average	74.2%	77%

As we compare the statistics, most parents would see District B as the better district. Schools 2, 4, and 5 have superior graduation rates. This implies they probably have more advanced courses and an abundance of resources. However, here is where the numbers get funny: District B has two extremely low-performing schools. Although the overall statistics for District B look very satisfying—in actuality District B may have the same raw number of students receiving diplomas as District A—the issue is that the quality of education is apparently different. District A has only fair-performing schools and District B has two extremely low-performing schools. These two schools in District B may go overlooked because of the success of the other high-performing schools in its district.

This is the scenario described by Noguera; overlooking low-performing schools is effortless as long as the numbers look good. The calculability of McDonaldization is quite clever and the goal is quantity over quality. Society ignores impoverished schools and the successful few are used to justify the entire system. Statistics are skewed in various ways to give the illusion of success.

In the American education system, productivity is equivalent to quality. Private and suburban schools are left to carry the weight of neutralizing the failure of poor and urban schools. So whose responsibility is it to handle the low-performing schools? Noguera says:

"Throughout the United States, failing schools are treated as local matters, and responsibility for improving them is delegated to those who reside in the communities they serve. This continues to be the case whether or not communities can generate the resources to address the needs of poor students" (13).

The communities in which these failing schools operate lack the financial backing to bring new technologies into classrooms, to buy new books, or to hire additional staff to reduce classroom sizes. Teachers in low-performing schools are either new and inexperienced or experienced but jaded by the poor working conditions. To put the burden on that particular community to fix the problem is ridiculous. In fact, the low-income community lacks the influence or capital to change its schools' problems.

Noguera says it best: *"As long as we are able to convince ourselves that simply providing access to education is equivalent to providing equal opportunity, we will continue to treat failing schools as a nonissue"* (15). Think about the example of District A and B. Which school needs more attention?

Standardized testing also illustrates how the McDonaldization principle of calculability has trickled into the classroom. The definition of a standardized test is a test administered and scored in a consistent or "standard" manner. It is constructed by specialists and experts based on standardized norms and principles. Experts decide the "norms" and standard principles used to determine the future of American children.

How often do these experts visit classrooms? Do they visit low-performing schools to determine the "norms"? Unless the norms of all types of schools are taken into consideration, there is nothing normal about a standardized test.

Furthermore, the assumption that all students who take the test are being exposed to the same curriculum and educational experience is untrue. Although there are standards or common core objectives to cover and predesigned steps to prepare students for the state objective test not all teachers implement these objectives at the same pace.

There are many reasons for this and it would be impossible to list them all here. Not all teachers approach lessons in a manner that engages students in the curriculum in a meaningful way. This is

CALCULABILITY

where professional development comes into play.

Professional development classes, in theory, are supposed to help teachers' performances as they perfect their craft. Unfortunately, teachers find themselves being assigned to multiple professional development classes that lack relevance for teaching today's children. These classes put "tricks in the teacher's bag" to help them prepare students to pass the standardized tests. Instead of focusing on innovation and creativity, many of these development classes have become calculated and predictable.

CHAPTER 4

Expecting the Predictable

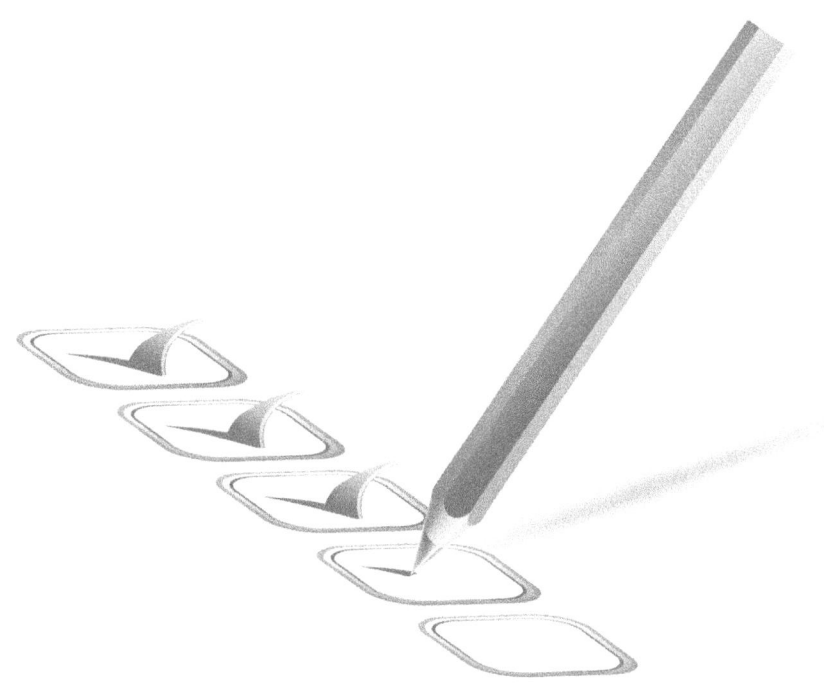

All school districts are evaluated by their state's department of public instruction. These evaluations are controlled by the current education reform laws in place on national and state levels. Reviews are rotated every few years and data is used for comparative purposes. Predictable scores are what states look for when evaluating the strength of districts and the performance of teachers.

Before we can discuss the predictability factor in the McDonaldization of schools let us first look at the history of education reform laws in the United States. This review will dissect a few of the laws, their goals, effects, and influence on society over the last century.

Plessy v. Ferguson (1896)[1]

Law	Goal	Outcome
Uphold segregation as long as each race enjoyed "separate but equal" facilities	Allowed segregation to continue in every facet of life including schools.	Continued disparity in the quality of education of minorities due to a lack of proper funding & resources; dilapidated buildings; outdated textbooks.

Smith-Hughes National Vocational Education Act (1917)[2]

Law	Goal	Outcome
Made federal funds available to train those entering agricultural work.	Boost agricultural productivity due to the demand in the marketplace at the turn of the century.	Taught students a trade but limited transference of skills into other ca-reers as society and the market changed; in-creased employment dislocation.

Brown v. Board of Education (1954)[3]

Law	Goal	Outcome
Deemed the "separate but equal" principle to be inherently unequal and unconstitutional; overruled Plessy v. Ferguson.	Remove racial barriers between minority and white students in the school system; make educational opportunities "equal".	Many schools remained segregated into the early 70s in the south, contributing to the gap in achievement between minorities and their white counterparts.

Elementary and Secondary Education Act (1965)[4]

Law	Goal	Outcome
Implemented as a part of Lyndon B. Johnson's "War on Poverty" to aid students from impoverished communities.	Shorten the achievement gap; provide extra funding for professional development and instruction; increase parental involvement	Title I schools developed; increased federal funds available to impoverished schools; poor to excellent execution of funds by school districts.

Education of the Handicapped Act (1975 & 1989)[5]

Law	Goal	Outcome
Made free, appropriate education available to all eligible students with a disability and use the word "disability" over the word "handicap".	To create equivalent educational experiences for physically and mentally challenged students just as regular students; give parents a say in the process.	Students with disabilities were often placed in separate settings with other disabled students; did not guarantee equal educational opportunities.

Individuals with Disabilities Education Act (1990 & 2004)[6]

Law	Goal	Outcome
Govern how states and public agencies provide early inter-vention and services for children with disabilities.	To ensure free and ap-propriate education is provided to students with disabilities; unique learning needs are met to age 21; en-sure that they are fu-ture-ready	Varied results across nation; lack of follow-through in intervention process; breaks in services provided; poorly written IEPs and 504 plans.[8]

No Child Left Behind Act (2001)[7]

Law	Goal	Outcome
Requires all govern-ment funded schools to give standardized tests; Title I schools must show Adequate Yearly Progress (AYP); military recruiters are provided access to contact students.	To increase accounta-bility of schools; measure student growth; ensure "highly qualified" teachers are provided to all stu-dents; allows military recruiters to obtain student contact infor-mation.	Holds a diversity of learners to one standardized test; sets standards that many schools have missed since it conception in 2001; teacher value tied to standardized test results; "teaching to the test" practice increases due to fear of failing scores versus teaching for intellectual develop-ment.

By taking a brief walk through education reform since the turn of the century, we can make certain comparisons and inferences regarding the impact of education reform laws on society. We see cycles of social injustice, continued failure to shorten the achievement gap, and unrealistic goal setting for teachers and administrators.

Plessy v. Ferguson made it legal to keep minorities and their white counterparts separated in every facet of life—where they lived, went to school, and even their access to wealth. Plessy v. Ferguson allowed the disparity of educational attainment to persist like a festering wound. Most urban neighborhoods where minorities lived lacked the wealth and resources of children in affluent neighborhoods. Schools in poor neighborhoods remained unsupported and the education of their children remained dangerously neglected.

This shortage in capital and power has remained an inherent characteristic of minority schools. As a result, the performance of students from these urban schools has remained subpar as compared to that of students in affluent schools. In the book, *Social Inequality*, the research of Susan Mayer explains this phenomenon: "There is some evidence that income inequality itself may be a risk for children…As income inequality increases, the educational attainment of low-income children declines while that of high-income children rises" (Neckerman 223).

The disproportionate distribution of wealth across neighborhoods of various socio-economic strata is a factor in the achievement gap. It inherently exposes high-income children to brighter educational futures and low-income children to educational woes. Sadly, this problem has been aggravated over the last century.

"Rising income inequality did indeed contribute to the increase in residential segregation by income and ethnicity between 1970 and 1990. During this period the poor were increasingly concentrated into urban neighborhoods that were largely populated by other poor people and ethnic minorities" (Wilson 1987, 1996; Massey and Eggers 1990; Massey and Denton 1993; Jargowsky 1997) (Neckerman 119).

Expecting the Predictable

Although Brown v. Board of Education (1954) overturned Plessy v. Ferguson, the aftereffects linger. This law does not support segregation by race but by economic background. Minority students are often exposed to schools with fewer resources than their white counterparts. This perpetuates the widening of the achievement and wealth gap.

The achievement gap is not just the burden or fault of the classroom teacher. It goes deep into the fabric of our society and whittles away at the faulty foundation of education we have been building upon.

The Smith-Hughes National Vocational Education Act of 1917 created vocational education. Federal funds were channeled into schools for teaching students trades in farm work. The funds for these educational programs were separate from the mainstream curriculum. Students were simply learning a trade, not developing cognitive thinking skills. At the turn of the century, there was an agricultural boom, making this act very successful at the time, but it lacked long-term vision. In the book, *Thinking for a Living: Education & the Wealth of Nations*, the authors comment:

"This Act strengthened the American economy of the time, but it sowed the seeds of problems to come. Those who labored had few choices. Employers saved money by recruiting line workers, college-educated women, and minorities who were willing to work for wages far below market value under strenuous working conditions" (Marshall & Tucker 22-23).

In the end, this act crippled immigrants, minorities, and women, preventing them from earning a substantial income. Without realizing it, they were signing up to be impoverished line workers who would have little say over their futures.

Some of the earliest effects of McDonaldization can be seen even before the establishment of the fast food industry itself, turning students into line and factory workers instead of critical thinkers and entrepreneurs. Schools became inadvertent accomplices in this process. Marshall and Tucker note:

"A whole system had been elaborated in the schools the purpose of which was to tell these line workers what to do and how to do it, factory style. It would be little wonder that intellectually able people who expected to think for themselves would flee the schools at the first opportunity..." (24).

With the full, federally mandated participation of schools, students were handicapped before entering the marketplace. Hard labor was the curriculum and not the understanding of innovative technology, medicine, science, or higher mathematics.

The Smith-Hughes Act of 1917 was a great solution to the agricultural demands of the country, but it took no thought for the future. This act was amended later. Unfortunately, however, the residual damage was too great to mend.

As the marketplace changed post World War II into the 70's, efficient technology emerged. The need for factory workers began to decline and the need for creativity to develop phones, radios, and computers increased.

Unable to find enough talented U.S. labor, jobs were shipped overseas to increase the profits of companies operating on American soil (Marshall & Tucker 32). The same students who were turned into factory workers found themselves unemployed. Their training, specific to trade work such as making uniforms, harvesting crops, or assembling cars, for example, left them unable to make career changes.

Expecting the Predictable

Although the post World War II market shifted to international trade and increased profitability, American workers found themselves unable to benefit. Uneducated assembly line workers were not trained to compete globally. International workers were better educated, innovative, and witty.

American companies had to find ways to keep costs low, constantly changing pricing to compete with foreign companies. Naturally, the first place to cut costs was labor (Marshall & Tucker 33).

Where could under-educated factory workers go to find work during times of technological advancement? The choices were limited. These limitations ultimately had an affect on the next generation. Children of unemployed factory workers had little access to a better education. With little to no income in the household, the cycle continued to widen the achievement gap between those with wealth, resources, and access to a good education and those who did not, a cycle called *pervasive systematic oppression.*

Education reform has a tendency to do the exact opposite of what it proposes. The purpose of educational reform should be to prepare students to compete globally. Still, these reforms systematically suppress groups of people, pushing them further down into their socio-economic classes.

The most recent education reform law, No Child Left Behind (2001), under the George W. Bush administration, has been one of great controversy. This law sought to tackle several objectives, but let us just focus on standardized testing. This law set the precedent that every child's progress must be assessed by a state-delivered, standardized test. Each year American children assemble in classrooms with pencils, scrap paper, and anxiety, ready to take one final test—a standardized test—with the potential to either promote them to the next grade or prevent it. The tests within each subject are the same and are supposed to assess the progress of each child, teacher, and school.

Although the tests are equal in content, they cannot fully depict a child's capabilities. We have already established in previous chapters that not all students receive an equal education due to socioeconomic circumstances, so how can a standardized test be equal?

Standardized tests are often labeled as culturally biased. In the book, *Battleground: Schools*, authors Mathison and Ross write:

"The bias in standardized test questions may be based on cultural, class, ethnic, gender, or linguistic differences. The increased use of standardized tests called high-stake tests, those where the results are used to make important decisions resulting in rewards or punishments, has, however, reinforced the disadvantages standardized tests present for students of color and living in poverty" (605).

Not only is the equity in standardized testing questionable, but its affects on test-takers creates much concern. According to a National Educational Longitudinal Survey, minorities and those living in poverty consistently score lower than their white counterparts score, have higher dropout rates, and experience unhealthy levels of anxiety associated with standardized testing (Mathison & Ross 605). There is no doubt that different groups perform extremely differently on standardized tests. It is not a matter of ability but rather exposure and access to information.

School effectiveness and people's jobs are based on predictable scores. As a result, teachers compete against one another rather than working together. If the numbers look right then

Expecting the Predictable

there are no worries for teachers. However, if the scores show more children struggling more than normal, that teacher will be closely scrutinized. Obviously, teacher competence is an important factor, but the teacher cannot be the *only* factor. One must consider differences in learning styles, family backgrounds, school quality, and availability of resources.

The No Child Left Behind Act of 2001 has made standardized testing the rule and not the exception. It has become another way for McDonaldization to infiltrate the school system. In the book, *Fast Food Nation*, Schlosser writes:

"Grades (and the students obsessed by this quantifiable measure of education) might be derived from a series of machine-graded, multiple-choice exams and posted impersonally, often by number rather than by name. In sum, students may feel like little more than objects into which knowledge is poured as they move along an information-providing and degree-granting educational assembly line" (161).

It is understandable that students often feel an unhealthy amount of anxiety when taking mandated tests. No Child Left Behind made their futures dependent upon successful completion. There is no way of guaranteeing an equal education for all students, so we cannot guarantee successful completion of standardized tests for all students.

Teachers are expected to churn out successful students regardless of socio-economic factors beyond their control. Yes, all children are inherently capable of succeeding, but it is presumptuous to imply that the skills for learning are consistent among students across the board. We now see children as a number with no personality—a predictable score. American education has placed more value on the score than the individual.

The laws discussed in this chapter show a variety of thoughts and ideas about how education should be transformed, yet they do not cohesively fit. This is confusing for students, teachers, and school administrations. Hargreaves writes: "Old waves and new waves of reforms create confusing cross-currents of change that can be difficult to navigate and that can even drag teachers under" (7). Consistency is needed so teachers can adjust to the necessary changes influencing the classroom. Before this can happen, policymakers have a responsibility to get in touch with the realities of the classroom. They must look beyond scores and into the eyes of the children being taught in order to help them.

---

[1] Public Law 163 U.S. 537, Plessy v. Ferguson (1896)

[2] Public Law 347. 64th Cong., 2d sess., February 23, 1917. Reprinted in *The Statutes at Large of the United States of America from December, 1915, to March, 1917.* Vol. 39, Part 1. Washington, D.C.: GPO, 1917, 929–936.

[3] Public Law 347 U.S. 483, Brown v. Board of Education of Topeka (1954)

[4] Public Law 89-10, 79 Stat. 27, 20 U.S.C. ch.70, The Elementary and Secondary Education Act (1965)

[5] Public Law 94-142 Education of the Handicapped Act (1975) & Pubic Law 101-476 Individuals with Disabilities Education Act (1989)

[6] Public Law 101-476 Individuals with Disabilities Education Act (1990) & Individuals with Disabilities Education Improvement Act of 2004, Public Law 108-446 (2004)

[7] Public Law 107-110 No Child Left Behind (2001)

[8] IEP = individualized Education Plan and 504 is a special education plan that caters to the individual needs of the qualified students receiving these services

CHAPTER 5

Who Is in Control?

Who Is in Control?

State governments and boards of education control what happens in schools. Very few of these political figures visit the classroom, and if they do so, it is irregularly. They remain "out of touch" with the struggles of schools and educators.

The error of government taking full control and leaving teachers out of the policy-making process has monumental consequences:

"Political and administrative devices for bringing about change usually ignore, misunderstand or override teacher's own desires for change. Such devices commonly rely on principles of compulsion, constraint, and contrivance to get teachers to change... The involvement of teachers in educational change is vital to its success, especially if the change is complex and is to affect many settings over long periods of time... Teachers are not just technical learners. They are social learners too" (Hargreaves, 11-14).

The critical turn needed to change education lies in the hearts and minds of its teachers. Who else is at the forefront of what is happening in the classrooms on a daily basis? Who experiences the progress and setbacks of education reform firsthand? It is classroom teachers. Without their valuable input government will continue to create new legislation capable of doing nothing more than missing the mark—again.

Teachers play a fundamental role not only in the psychological development of children, but also in their social development. We coach them on teamwork, acceptance, responsibility, organization, and citizenship. These vital contributions alone qualify teachers to participate in the politics of education. However, barriers prevent teachers from taking an active role in the policy-making process: (1) The use of administrators to micromanage classrooms, and (2) A culture of conformity.

Many teachers lose their voices in the noise of bureaucracy and these two factors contribute to control over teachers.

Micromanagement

Formal observations are used to assess the effectiveness of teachers. Administrators hold teachers accountable through these observations. However, unfair or excessive evaluations can create environmental pressures that only serve to stress teachers.

Administrators' feedback can be biased: It is their point of view of what a successful classroom looks like. Apart from a repetitive history of student failure, a formal action plan, or excessive parent-student complaints, a teacher's effectiveness is based solely on one individual's opinion. Who is accountable for assessing the validity of such evaluations? Can an observer's information be considered always unbiased, ethical, and reliable?

Current evaluation instruments provide little insight into the full range of capabilities of a teacher. They tell even less about the atmosphere of a classroom on a daily basis. The issues surrounding current teacher evaluation processes are connected to the widget effect.

The *widget effect* can be defined as the failure of evaluation systems to provide accurate and credible information about individual teachers' instructional performance (Weisburg et al, 4). A report presented by the New Teacher Project highlights the flaws of the current system and makes suggestions to improve it. The current system:

- Assumes all teachers are good and perform the same,
- Ignores the work of excellent teachers,
- Provides minimal guidance and support to novice and

non-tenured teachers,
- Leaves underdeveloped teachers without proper feedback,
- Does not assign professional development classes that specifically tie into the areas where growth is needed,
- Does not guarantee a fair hearing and low-stakes upon dismissal,
- Does not ensure that all administrators have received extensive and proper training to provide accurate, fair, and competent feedback on evaluation instruments,
- Assumes more frequent visits to the classroom and thorough evaluations will provide a more accurate assessment of the teacher and boost the teacher's confidence about the process,
- Provides teachers with infrequent administrator feedback (Weiss et al. 18-22).

Evaluations should be used to develop teachers, and for those who may not be suited to the profession, to help them leave with dignity. Micromanagement through excessive evaluation and observations cannot accomplish this. Teachers must be able to improve in areas of weakness with attendance to professional development classes that address those areas.

Administrators and teachers must dialogue about areas of strength and weakness on a more frequent basis to prevent low rate evaluations. The assumption that high traffic into a teacher's classroom will develop the teacher must be put to rest.

A Culture of Conformity

McDonaldization seeks to control the individual and make

individuals conform to the whole. The threat of individuality to a corporation is best described by Ray Kroc: "...*The organization cannot trust the individual; the individual must trust the organization*" (Schlosser 5). From the point of view of administration, there is no need for teachers to complain or take problems upstream if everyone, as a team, conforms to the same set of rules. All teachers are expected to perform at the same level, fulfill their extra duties, and volunteer more of their personal time with no compensation.

Individualism is frowned upon. The use of non-traditional means of teaching (games, pop music, art, debate teams, etc) in core curriculum classes like math and science tends to be looked down upon. These methods are more accepted in low-performing, urban schools.

There is no simple answer as to why this is true, but it is evident that collaborative, research-based efforts are favored over creative, self-developed methods. Hargreaves writes:

"Well-intentioned drives to create collaborative cultures and to expunge the culture of teacher isolation and individualism are in serious danger of eliminating individuality among teachers, and with it the disagreeable creativity that can challenge administrative assumptions and be a powerful force for change" (17).

No one is suggesting a chaotic situation where there are no teacher boundaries. Absolutely, there have to be standards for teaching. Thorough research and gap analysis can provide the right parameters, but not at the expense of ingenuity and originality. If our goal is to prepare children to compete globally, creating a uniform learning experience from classroom to classroom is not ideal for developing great thinkers and problem-solvers.

Who Is in Control?

Teachers who teach from the heart find joy in helping children prepare for life. This joy, unfortunately, can be overshadowed by rules, procedures, and policies that restrict it. Gold & Roth writes,

"The joy of helping others grow and watching them mature is dampened, even destroyed, by the growing tensions, stultifying conditions and unrealistic demands on teachers... The disillusionment experienced by teachers has become a mark of the profession" (1).

This type of control is what pushes good teachers out of the profession, new talented teachers and veterans alike. The following diagram demonstrates what happens as policy is handed down. This is called, the *hierarchy of control.*

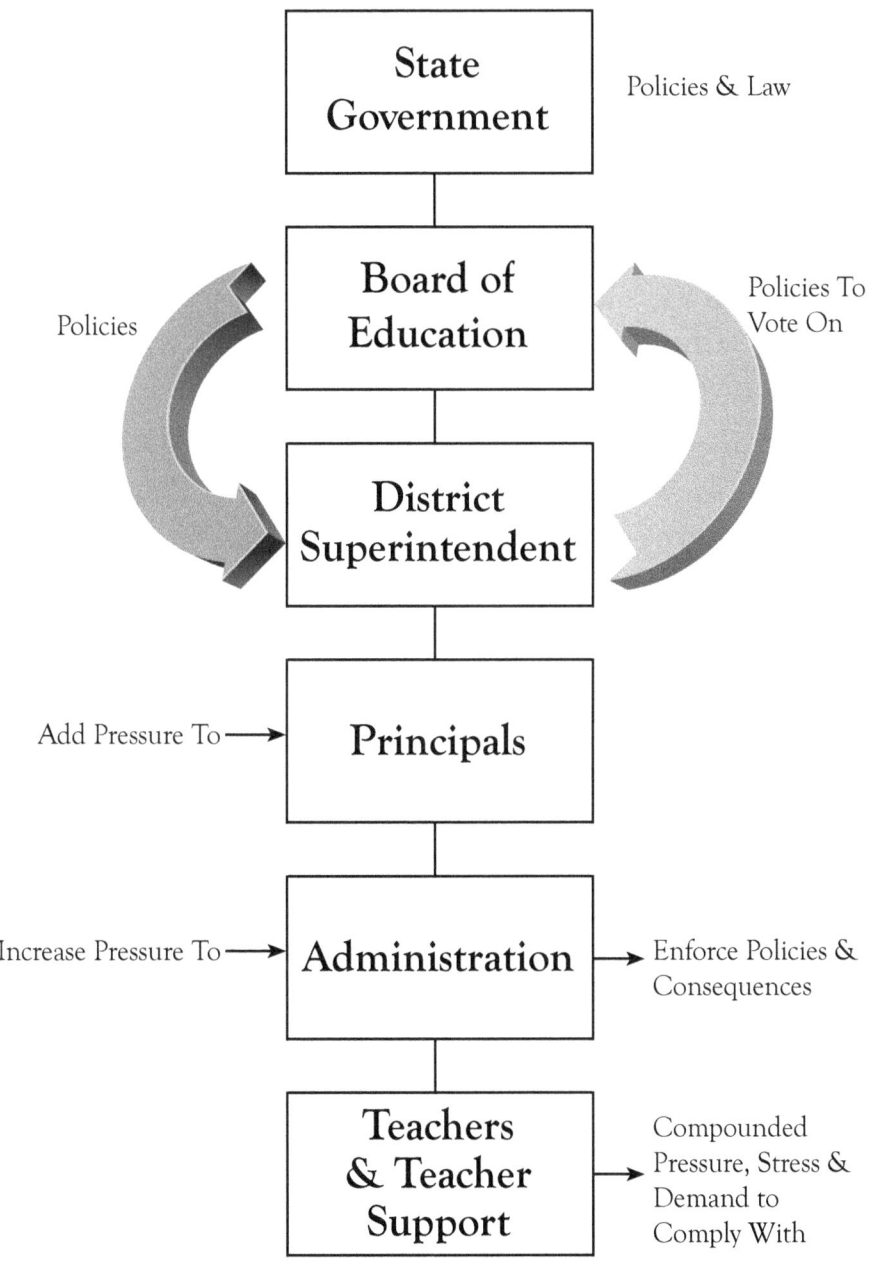

Who Is in Control?

State governments create education reform laws based on the U.S. Department of Education. State policies trickle down to the Board of Education, which oversees the District Superintendent. Then there is a very interesting exchange between the Board of Education and District Superintendent. Although the Board of Education has the power to impose its authority over the District Superintendent, most times the Board is controlled by the political influence of the District Superintendent. The Board of Education has the right to vote "Yea" or "Nay" on any policy proposed by the District Superintendent. Yet often it is overruled by the influence and power of the District Superintendent.

District Superintendents apply pressure to principals to push their schools to meet state-mandated goals. This pressure is passed down to administration (assistant principals and administrative staff) who have the most direct contact with teachers. Administrators perform most of the managerial work—making observations, attending parent-teacher meetings, and enforcing policies and consequences.

Teachers experience the compounded effect of this pressure and control since they are at the bottom of the hierarchy. Vandenbergh and Huberman call this process the external locust of control. Politicians and administrators set unrealistic policies in place and expect teachers to meet these goals (34). When you add it all up, teachers feel a loss of power and a lack of importance.

Let us illustrate how McDonaldization uses the ingredients of control, excessive paperwork, heavy workload, low wages, and lack of mobility to create a perfect mix for frustration and burnout among teachers. Try not to get lost in the sarcasm used in this illustration. Pay close attention to how the ingredients are placed and where the teacher is situated amidst all of it.

McDonaldization Combo #1:
The Burnout Sandwich for Teachers

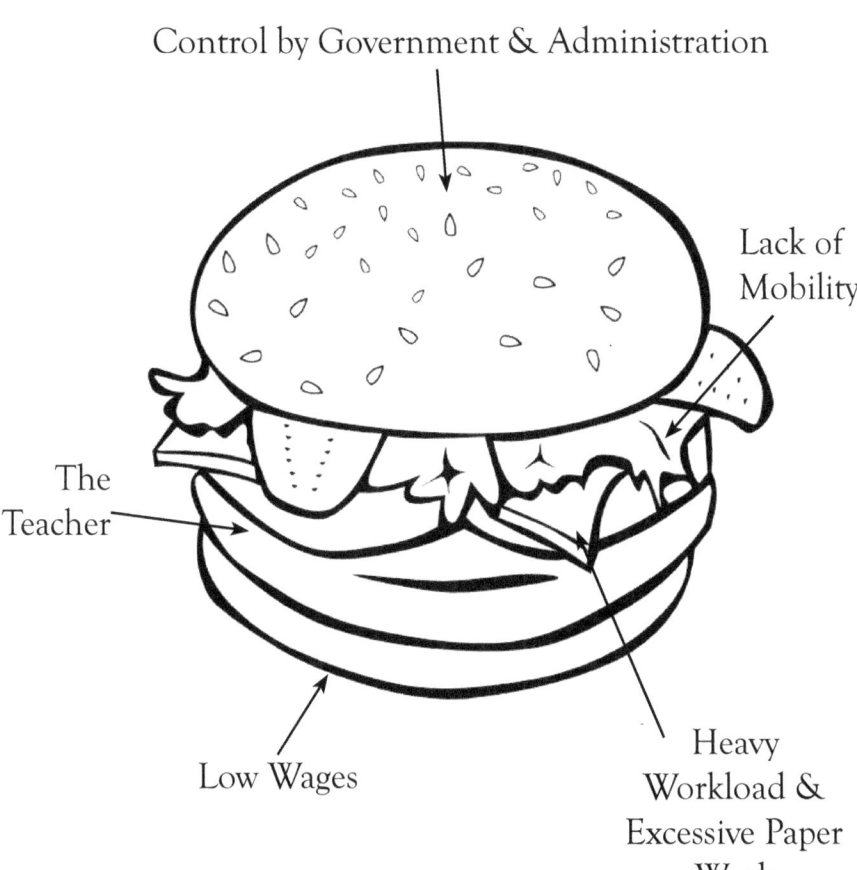

CHAPTER 6

Recommendations

Recommendations

Of what value is a book full of complaints with no solutions? Chapters 1-5 provide the basis for the following recommendations, which I believe, can help us move forward in reforming education. The goal is to revisit our "think tank" and have policy-makers, educators, and communities work together in redefining the education system.

Redefine Roles

Student-Teachers are defined as:

- Teachers in training enrolled in a college as an Education major;
- Committed to two years of teaching internships at schools of varied socioeconomic backgrounds;
- Trained in school documentation and procedures;
- Shadowing an administrator for an agreed amount of time to understand the administration of schools.

Novice teachers are defined as:

- Teachers with 0-5 years of experience or career-changers entering the profession;
- Having a restriction of no more than 50% of teaching assignments containing high percentages of high-needs students (first year);
- Assigned to a quality mentor who meets with them on a weekly basis (mentors must have documented success and allow mentee to observe them teaching on an ongoing basis in first year of service);

- Assigned professional development specific to lesson planning, creative learning techniques, and classroom management.

Master teachers are defined as:

- Teachers with a Master's degree;
- With six or more years of experience;
- Having documented ability to teach a variety of classes.

Resource Assistants should:

- Be placed in classrooms containing 33% or more of below-grade-level performers;
- Have special education backgrounds;
- Provide individual coaching;
- Be available for co-teaching opportunities;
- Be responsible for creation of Personalized Education Plans;
- Solicit teachers' input.

Planning committees within content areas should:

- Allow everyone to share in decision-making;
- Allow for common planning;
- Leave room for individuality and creativity;
- Set guidelines for enrollment in courses offered;
- Submit guidelines to guidance departments.

Recommendations

Lack of Mobility

Remove the glass ceiling by:

- Consistently rotating teacher assignments;
- Eliminating seniority and providing equal opportunity for all teachers;
- Requiring every teacher to share the responsibility of teaching classes with high percentages of below-grade-level performers.

Define the selection criteria for choosing a department chairperson:

- Candidates must take an apprenticeship where training is documented for at least one full school year;
- Candidates should have a time limitation on the number of years they can serve.

Provide professional development that offers skills transferable to other professions to:

- Allow entrance into other professions if the teacher decides to exit education;
- Increase marketability of teachers in the marketplace.

Excessive Paper Work and Heavy Load

Create partnerships with community organizations to provide administrative, clerical, and teacher assistance.

- This may include parents, student teachers, retired teachers, teacher assistants, substitutes, community leaders, and coaches, etc.

Make scheduling and class recommendations strictly the role of the Guidance Department.

- Follow planning committee's guidelines for enrollment.
- Make class recommendation forms available electronically.
- Allow teachers the option of changing recommendations.

Locker assignments and payment collections should be assigned to secretarial/clerical staff or a volunteer committee.

Curriculum and Content

Allow teachers as well as principals to nominate individuals to participate in the state curriculum-planning process.

- Select individuals to attend rigorous curriculum development training.

Assure that curriculum promotes global and interdisciplinary views.

- Partner with local businesses, corporations, and colleges/universities.
- Integrate internships into core courses.
- Initiate student-business mentor relationships.
- Invite speakers on a rolling basis.
- Incorporate periods of sustained silent reading.
- Provide resource assistants for literacy services to students who read below grade level and English-as-a-second-language learners (ESL).
- Make courses career- and technology-guided.
- Provide lessons that develop a "think and do" approach, not fact regurgitation.

Integrate math and reading into every core course specific to curriculum content.

Recommendations

- Co-teach traditional math and English and share roster with curriculum teacher.
- Create an interdisciplinary approach to content.
- Help students become less overwhelmed.
- Make math relevant and applicable to career choices.
- Drive literacy across content areas.

Change grade level promotion requirements.

- Administer three smaller district tests rather than one standardized state test at the end of the year.
- Base credits on successful completion of tests, internships, and an academic portfolio.
- Require participation in off-site Saturday classes for failure to meet standards until requirements are met.
- End social promotion.

Change Core Curriculum Courses to:

Government and Civil Service

- Politics
- Law
- Business and Economics
- Society and Culture
- Global Competition
- Logic 1 & 2 (elements of Algebra 1 & 2), Data Analysis, Statistics and Function Modeling

Technology
- Computer Technology
- Engineering
- Logic 1 & 2, Geometry, Pre Calculus, and Calculus, Statistics and Function Modeling

Humanities
- Psychology
- Sociology
- Art and History
- Philanthropy
- Logic 1 & 2, Geometry, Data Analysis

Biomedical Field
- Health and Medicine
- Food and Nutrition
- Research Methods
- Anatomy
- Breakthroughs in medical research
- Logic 1 & 2, Geometry, Pre Calculus, Calculus, Statistics and Function Modeling

Entrepreneurship & Business
- Business Planning
- Banking & Finance
- Marketing/Advertising
- Asset and Debt Management

Recommendations

- Community Development
- Elements of Grant Writing
- Logic 1 & 2, Geometry, Data Analysis
- Building a non-for profit

Enforce a required placement test in transition from middle school to high school.

- Provide correct placement and reduction in student stress.

Compensation

Institute a minimum wage of $40,000 with bonus opportunities and annual raises.

- Offer small bonuses for each strong evaluation.
- Offer tuition reimbursement for Masters in Education (career-changers).
- Encourage people from diverse backgrounds to enter the field.
- Offer increased bonus rates to Master Teachers.
- Offer up to six figure incomes with documented success over time and tenure.

Observations and Other Protocols

Institute three formal observations per school year:

- One conducted by non-administrative Master Teacher (with more than 10 years experience);
- One conducted by the Head Principal;
- One conducted by an Assistant Principal.

Accompany all formal observers with a person from the school's volunteer committee.

- Reduce biased ratings by having evaluations of administrators or master teachers cross-examined by committee volunteers.

Hold post-evaluation meetings with teachers to discuss results.

- Encourage teachers to attend professional development classes relevant to their areas of weakness.
- Compensate teachers for exceptional observations.
- Allow rebuttals to low-ratings to be examined by trained "on-site" human resources professionals—individuals with teaching experience and HR training.

Make sure observation reports are comprehensive and address:

- Teaching style
- Demographics of the class observed
- Classroom climate
- Lesson structure and student interaction
- Tracking of students' academic achievement
- Colleague feedback
- Self-Assessments
- Portfolio Work

Allow teachers, in turn, to evaluate administrators and principals.

- Create a system of checks and balances.
- Conduct/collect information by a third-party source.
- Protect anonymity.

Recommendations

Limit informal observations to low-performing teachers and all first year teachers.

- Allow due process for teachers who consistently perform low after professional development by in-person hearings.
- Administer layoff for low poor performance, not termination. (Substantial evidence is needed for termination and is reserved for more serious offenses.)

Distribution of Wealth and Control

Apply directly for state funding based on:

- School status
- Title I
- Free/reduced lunch statistics
- Capital strength of school neighborhood
- Surplus or deficit from previous year
- Spending patterns
- Average classroom size
- Available Resources

Decentralize district personnel to:

- Reduce bureaucracy that teachers encounter on state and local levels;
- Increase decision-making ability of administration, teachers, and community;
- Boost cost efficiency;
- Make schools accountable to Board of Education directly on ethical issues, performance, and stewardship of state funding;

- Have district personnel on-site in schools, acting as a third party for checks and balances;
- Place on-site Human Resources centers in each school.

Use resources for supplies, salaries, services, learning materials, classroom technology, energy costs, professional development, and tutors.

- Have reports on school's use of funds prepared by on-site district personnel.
- Give teachers equal input on school budget.

Give teachers voting privileges in final steps of education reform policies on the state level.

- Make regular visits by State officials to schools so that they stay "in touch" with realities at each school.

Allow Unlimited Creativity

Debate teams and group discussions:

- Help children develop public speaking skills;
- Teach students to think critically and challenge others to think critically.

Subject Jeopardy:

- Creates a sense of teamwork and organization.

Poster-board projects with rubrics:

- Enforce literacy;
- Require organizations skills.

Interactive notebooks and scrapbooking:

- Encourage creativity;

Recommendations

- Help students personalize the note-taking process.

Curriculum spin on traditional games:

- Creates fun and interest.

Scavenger Hunts:

- Help children think logically and match items.

Group Presentations:

- Encourage teamwork;
- Require delegation of responsibilities;
- Develop leadership skills.

Journaling and Reflection Logs:

- Allow students to connect new information with prior knowledge.

Music Therapy:

- Helps soothe anxiety to facilitate focus on work.

The Socratic Method:

- Boosts critical thinking skills.

Error Analysis:

- Encourages critical thinking;
- Helps with organization;
- Reinforces concepts learned.

Work Stations:

- Enable students to work together;
- Allow reasonable amounts of socialization.

Websites:

- Develop communication skills.

Manipulatives and Arts & Crafts:

- Facilitate the hands-on approach to assessment for kinesthetic learners.

Skits and Role Playing:

- Increase creativity and student interaction.

Videos:

- Provide a more acceptable form of lecturing for children.

Food:

- Provides opportunities to develop the whole person.

Student-created Assessments:

- Allow students a more active role in their learning experiences.

Student-to-teacher Interviews:

- Reduce stress in the classroom and provide mentoring opportunities.

Technology in Every Classroom

    Access to Wi-Fi.

    Flat screen TVs for educational programs/movies

    Promethean Boards/Smart Boards

    Laptops or iPad labs

    Educational apps for cell phones, Androids, and iPhones

    Touch screen tutorials

Recommendations

Reading and Math Labs for struggling performers provided throughout the day

School Music Network as music therapy with preapproved music

Teachers are facilitators of knowledge and not just lecturers. We are competing every day with cutting-edge technologies and must be equally relevant in order to keep the attention of today's youth. To reach this generation, we must be willing to make necessary changes as other countries have done. If we do not, we may one day find ourselves an impoverished nation.

About the Author

Bridgette Jackson is a freelance writer and member of the Writers Café. As CEO and Founder of the Charlotte 1st Organization, which is dedicated to community development as well as improving educational quality for impoverished individuals, she is an ardent child advocate. Jackson is an educator with several years of teaching experience in the states of Virginia and North Carolina in mainstream, private, and alternative school settings. With such a diverse background in education, she has influenced children of many backgrounds and learning differences. She is known to be passionate about improving the American educational system for the sake of tomorrow's generations. Jackson currently resides in Charlotte, North Carolina, amid family and friends.

There is growing discontent among teachers in America. The "microwave mentality" has seeped into the classroom. With all the unrealistic expectations placed on classroom teachers many have become disenchanted, disengaged, and sadly, a large percentage are leaving the profession.

www.ingramcontent.com/pod-product-compliance
Lightning Source LLC
LaVergne TN
LVHW051153080426
835508LV00021B/2603